Lotus

Rackhouse Publishing

Read to Learn, Write to Remember

ISBN-13: 979-8-9853939-5-8

For information about custom editions, special sales, premium and bulk purchases, please contact:
Rackhouse Publishing
Rackhousepublishing@mail.com

First Edition

Printed in the U.S.A

Dedication

I dedicate this work to my heavenly father for being the head of my life and loving me no matter what. To my children, my mother Chandra, my grandmother Mary, my aunt Cynthia, to all my uncles and other relatives for always encouraging me to go through with my plans no matter what, always stay true to myself and keep God first.

I love you all!

xo, Rida

Acknowledgements

Writing this book has been so monumental for me and I want to take a moment to acknowledge a few people who have played an undeniable role in its completion. I don't want to miss anyone here so if you do not see your name, please charge it to my excitement and not my heart.

Special thanks to:

My first-born son, Christian Richardson, for believing in my ability to tell my story and reminding me every day to make sure I dedicate my time to my book. I thank you for being one of the biggest helpers I could ever ask for. You have been there for your sibling's day in and day out since day one and I'm super proud of you, son. I pray God gives you what's rightfully yours and the desires of your heart. I pray that you allow God to keep you guided and on the straight path. You're growing into an amazing young man.

Nikki Burnett for being a mentor/sister to me. Thanks for introducing me to a group of beautiful, empowered women. (CEO chicks)

Nicole McCall for pointing me in the right direction and being so supportive of me, getting my story out to reach others.

Melynda Rackley and the entire Rackhouse Publishing team for being there to coach me through the process of telling my story, encouraging me to stay true to my story and keep writing no matter what, while being the best publisher at the same time.

To my very special loved one for being there every step of the way through the process, may you continue to be blessed, abundantly!

I would like to reflect on the past and also thank everyone. The good and the bad who played a part in me becoming the best version of me, a queen. Thanks for helping me straighten up my crown. Everything helped me and will continue, helping me remain humble and in peace.

Last but certainly not least, I must thank myself for being strong enough to keep going and being gentle with myself.

I wrote a book! My dreams are now a reality!

CONTENTS

Introduction

The willingness to write this book came to me one summer of 2011. Almost out of nowhere, a lady approached me and told me everything that was going on in my life was for a reason and not to overthink things. I was sitting on a bench at the mall in front of the nail salon when this sweet lady sat down next to me. She commented on how hot it was outside and we exchanged smiles. Shortly before she sat down, I had just finished thinking about all the things I wanted and didn't have. She looked at me and spoke volumes that day. She told me everything going on in my life was for a reason and not to worry, just to trust the process. I didn't understand the reason she even said anything to me. She must have seen the look of confusion on my face, but it did not stop her. Eventually she explained to me how she was writing about her life and the challenges she overcame. I began to tell her how she inspired me. At that moment I remembered and voiced aloud that I wanted to write a book for a while, but I didn't know how to start. She told me to put God first and just do it, and it would work out. That seed was planted more than ten years ago but it does not matter how long it takes to achieve a goal. The thing that matters most is getting it done, and that's just what I did!

This has not been an easy path and while writing this I experienced some of my greatest challenges. I started this book after a major life change while constantly thinking about where I would be in six months. I was consumed with what I need to commit to and facing things I wanted to let go of. For the first time in my life, I was up close and personal with myself. I was ready to look at the things I wanted to forget and focused on my personal and financial growth. I was focused on where I desired to be financially in six months with an awareness of my attitude and outlook. That mattered because I knew there needed to be some adjustments in how I saw myself in order to achieve the goals I set. I needed to surrender, trust, rebirth and get away from people that didn't mean me any good. Shedding people can be tough, but it has happened in my past and will respectfully happen in my future. I have learned to accept the lessons as people leave. Writing this book allowed me to have a safe space to digest my thoughts, habits, dreams and mistakes. Again I say, this is not easy but I embrace it with the understanding that this is what I asked for.

I didn't even think it was possible to write this book and I'm now able to render my testimony unto others. The best part was my pain turning into purpose. I'm grateful for the pain I went through because I'm able to stand here now and it makes me a better person, but it isn't easy! The things we say to ourselves in our minds are so important and I saw this clearer than ever on the path to completing this. Some days it felt like I'd been thrown in the game by a coach, and I never was told what I was subbing for. I had to get up early in the morning while everyone was asleep just to get this done because there were so many random distractions. That's how I know this is meant to be. When you want something as bad as I wanted to write this book, you'd figure out a way to get it done too.

When I finished writing I felt so much joy in my heart because I did what I set out to do. I didn't let the seed that was planted in 2011 die. I remembered the joy and freedom the woman talking to me that day had. I made it my mission to one day emerge with confidence and freedom like her. Sometimes life is messy like an unpaved road after a bad rainstorm. The tears I have cried over the years made a puddle of pain in my heart, but I was ready for something beautiful to come from that.

When I made the call to my publisher, I knew I didn't want to carry my pain packed away inside holding me back anymore. I wanted to break the chains and reimagine a life with good things coming from the messy situations in my past. That one thought and having a conversation with my mother encouraged me to do a little bit of research. I discovered the lotus flower. The lotus emerges from the mud as a beautiful flower each day and even though there is muddy water underneath it, there is no mud on the surface. It is usually in perfect condition regardless of the dirt around, in or even underneath it. It emerges by using the nutrients from the water and dirt. That spoke to me! If a flower can use the messy conditions to be beautiful, so can I!

I want to challenge you to read my story with a mind that wants to emerge from any mess that may have happened to you in your past. I share journal entries from the months I spent writing and I encourage you to journal your thoughts as well. Writing is such an empowering activity, and you don't need any special education to do it. I have emerged as a confident woman during this process and that is rejuvenating. You have the power within you to restore, reinvent, reimagine and rejuvenate yourself too! I hope that reading this plants a seed just like meeting that stranger outside of the mall did for me. No matter what, don't ever give up on your dreams. The messy things in and around you are supposed to help you grow!

"The lotus emerges from the mud as a beautiful flower each day and even though there is muddy water underneath it, there is no mud on the surface...If a flower can use the messy conditions to be beautiful, so can I!

-Sherida

1

Determined To Be Me

May 10th, 2022 5 a.m.

I've been having so many blockages which have kept me from writing and expressing myself. It's five o'clock in the morning and I'm feeling much better than I have for months. I've been all over the place with my emotions. I guess I've been going through necessary growing pains. But as a human, it's always easier said than done. When you tell yourself it's gonna be alright. When you know things have to happen, to remember, to stay humble, to operate in love, to forgive, to be careful with yourself and your loved ones. Trouble came for me in all angles this past couple weeks and months, and I felt like just giving up.

It started with my dream career. I know nothing in life is easy, nor will it be easy to achieve my goals. Truth is some of the things that I have experienced in life hurt the most. I had been so pumped up about the fact of me going to take my real estate exam. I knew the test was coming up and was still trying to maintain my everyday life with my three kids.

They are all totally different with different personalities I have to juggle. I try to give more time to each one and keep track of the one that may need more than the other each week. Then juggling my overthinking and trying to keep myself in a positive space. All of this while trying to write a book! I want my dream career so badly, but more than that I want better for myself and my kids. I want them to have some things and experiences that I didn't. Growing up my life was tough. I want life to be easier, it's got to get better than this.

♡ Rida

This journey called life for me, started in a small town called Carrollton, Alabama, which to me was a small box where every African-American still to this day is under privileged if you ask me. My very first place I ever lived out of many places was located in a popular apartment complex where everyone knew each other. As for me, Sherida I am the first child out of four.

My very first friend in the world lived across the street from me. She was so sweet to me although her mom always looked at me funny. I imagine it was because my parents were always yelling and screaming at each other. I'm certain they could hear them across the street. I normally got disciplined for sneaking out with my friend to the playground without permission. I understood the reason why my dad disciplined me. I was very determined from the time I started walking. I wanted control of my own life. I wanted to be my own person. My family can contest that. My grandpa compared me to Rita Hayward, a famous, glamorous and talented actor. She was very determined, too. I had a great determination to do whatever.

My friend was like a sister to me. I remember when we were on the playground one day, we saw these men walking in what appeared to be white gowns. We noticed them first, and once they saw us they put on their white hoods. they looked like ghosts, that traumatized me. I didn't know why they had that on but I know I ran for my life. Not to even look back to see if my friend ran or not. I later learned what that was about and it terrified me to know that people were hated for the color of their skin. I went to tell my mom, but I'm not even sure if she believed me. She knew I had a big, creative imagination.

I was a kid that would ask like 101 questions from any adult. My mom didn't want me to mention that to anyone about the sheet wearing people. I didn't ask anyone other than my friend. She said she remembered seeing that and we never mentioned it again. We shortly moved away from the apartment only to leave my friend. We moved into a house across town, where you could hear and smell the sawmill. Not far from the school and also close to my house.

My mom and dad never really created any good memories for me together in that house. All I could remember was fighting, drinking and cursing. My mom didn't drink, but she had to fight my dad a lot. When I was a kid, he was the meanest person to my mom. I was always glad for my grandma to pick me up and take me home with her. Although I wasn't around any kids my age, I could still ask 1,001 questions.

My grandma lived right outside the town of Carrollton. I always enjoyed the ride in her 1975 Ford LTD. I would always ride with my arm out the window enjoying the wind hitting my face. I would close my eyes and use my imagination to take me where I wanted to be. The ride was always long for me. I knew on the way to my grandma's house we would pass by her church on the left and my granddad's house was on the right. I was always excited to get there and see my oldest cousin. She was an only child and I was her annoying little cousin. My grandma was walking distance from her house right in front of each other.

The small dirt road separated her house from my grandma's. And the main road was big as a matchbox. Her dad was one of my heroes growing up, but he didn't know it. I never told him. He called me cutin Rita B. Soon, as we would pull up in the yard, I would take off across the street to see my cousin. I know they must have hated to see me coming. Her mom was always on the couch watching as the world turned and guiding lights. She would be on the phone with a cord long enough for you to jump rope with. She was always gossiping about the shows she was watching. I would always go rambling in my cousins belongings. I would hear her saying stop that! Don't touch that! Put that back! I was always so fascinated with all the things she had that I never did.

She always had the prettiest fingernail polish, puzzles, and games. She also had a tall piggy bank full of change, and it would count the money automatically. She had mostly silver change and to me that was a lot of money. I never even had a piggy bank. Her dad would make homemade ice cream for us on weekends.

I was always asking what's that? How do you do that? Why do you do that? He would always answer me, no matter what. I would follow him in the yard everywhere he went too. My cousin had two bikes so I would use one of hers to follow her dad when she was tired of me. I would ride the bike and park it like it was a car. We would walk up the hill where he kept his work truck. He was a logger and he raised chickens and hogs. I was fascinated with helping him feed the chickens and the hogs. My cousin was too pretty for that. She would never go with us.

I would go to the top of the hill by the hogs sometimes on the bike and fly down the hill wide open with no hands thinking I was doing big things. I thought I was ready for my very own car. My grandma would call me in at the end of the day to help her wash peas and greens.

And I wanted no part in that. I only wanted to cut the lemons for her to put in the tea, which she wasn't having. My grandma lived in the house with our great aunt. She had Alzheimer's disease and my grandmother was her caregiver. She had children but they barely came around. Only my uncle across the street. It was mainly my grandma who took excellent care of her. She was definitely a pretty older woman. I always said she looked like an Indian with a big mole on her nose. She had long pretty white hair and my grandma would always keep it up for her. I soon started trying to play in her hair, but she would curse me out for messing with her head. I knew she didn't mean any harm.

My grandma was my biggest help. Most of the time with

school work and church stuff. She did that for me throughout my childhood during the little time my mom let me spend with her. She worked at the school, so she was always making laminated things for me to use at home to continue to learn. I was always excited to see what she brought home from school for me to use. We would mostly work on it when I would see her on the weekends. We would sit at the kitchen table to go over everything she brought me. My grandma was a multitasker, always cooking, cleaning and taking care of my great aunt while still helping me at the same time. She always kept it nice and clean. I had some of the best times at my grandma's house. Right along with her mouthwatering cooking. I looked forward to her fried pork chops or fried chicken with squash, collard greens, and candy yams topped off with homemade sweet tea.

After dinner, I would always go outside and sit in the old, rusted swing and day dream about my favorite show, which was the Barney show. I loved Barney so much I had a Barney teddy bear. I always said I was going to be on the show one day. On some weekends, my grandma would let me go to my dad's house to visit. The weekends there were totally different. Nothing like the weekends with my grandma on my mom's side of the family. I was so happy when Fridays came and I knew my dad was gonna pick me up.

I would sit in the sunroom and look out the window to watch for his car to pull up. My grandma would say a quick prayer with me and wait for my dad to get out and greet everyone. My mom never wanted my grandma to let me go. So my grandma would let him know to have me back at home on time, on Sunday's evening. I knew I was in my dad's hometown when we would bypass this big tree to lean over towards the road.. My dad would stop by the only store in the town and get my favorite snacks because he didn't want me asking anyone for anything. I always got my regular dill pickle chips, beef jerky, and Sprite snack.

We would pass the fire station and I knew we'd arrived at my grandma's house on my dad's side of the family. Everyone would be hanging around in the yard, drinking, laughing, playing cards, cooking on the grill, or even frying fish, other kids running around in the yard. And there was my cousin who was a year older than me on my dad's side. He would be ready for me to get out of the car so he could show me all his new things. He was always ready to compete with me or show me something new his mom and dad bought for him. He was my grandma's favorite plus he was spoiled. He was always pampered. The things I would get cursed out about and a whopping for his parents would just tell him, don't do that. Let me turn around and do the same thing he did and HELL would break loose. My dad would scream SHERIDA , get your butt over here and get the switch right now.

And don't get a little one because he was going to go get a bigger one. My uncles would yell at him don't whoop her like that and my dad would say, that's my child! Boy, he would beat me like I stole some and make me go lay down on my grandma's couch. My cousin would still be outside, enjoying himself. My dad was really mean to me and he never thought he was at all. He treated me the way he was treated.

My cousin would come into the house and peep around the corner and stick his tongue out at me and laugh. I would yell at him, leave me alone crybaby! My dad would be standing outside of the house, talking with his friends and yelling in there at me, screaming SHERIDA don't make me come back in there! I always just laid on the couch and cried. I was so ready to go home after those kinds of situations. He would come in and ask me what's wrong, boo? Like he didn't just whip my ass. I had whelps from the top of my arms to the bottom of my feet all over me. I would tell him I was ready to go home. He would take me home. Most of the time I would cry silently all the way home. I didn't want him to hear me crying. He would look over at me and see me cry and would tell me don't cry, baby. I'm sorry, Daddy sorry. You can't be acting up like that at grandma's house. I would just cry even more. I knew then that no matter what I ever did, he was going to whoop me for it.

One Saturday, I was back over my grandma's house on my dad's side and me and my cousin were riding bikes. And my dad would tell me, don't go out in the yard until my uncles would tell him, let her be a kid. He would yell, well don't go past that fire station! My big-headed cousin would pick on me cause he could go across the highway and I couldn't. He challenged me that particular day. He said, "I'm going to the red store and to the basketball court with my other cousins."

I said, "What other cousin?"

He replied, "My boy cousins."

That pissed me off. I knew in my mind I was going across that highway that day no matter what. I was determined and said I'm going too! He would say, "your daddy gonna whoop you."

I said, "So he's gonna whoop me anyways."

I looked back and saw what he was doing. He was standing around the fire, talking about the Cowboys football team, which was my dad's favorite team. He was always the loudest in the bunch. I knew they had his focus so I could take off. I got on that bike and hauled it to the store. Before I got off the bike he was coming across the road with the switch in his hand, peeling off the extra pieces.

My cousin was saying, "Ooh wee, Sherida you bout to get a whooping!"

He whooped me all the way back across the highway, without the bike. I proved my point to my cousin that day. Those whoopings made me super angry inside. After that day, I didn't visit again for a while. I started going back to my mom's for the weekend. We lived in the projects in town. I was so happy to get home with my mom. I remember days like skipping rocks in the creek behind the apartment and playing with kids in the neighborhood.

We would do all kinds of fun stuff in the projects. I was always thinking I was tough and it wasn't like I had a choice. My dad made me that way. At school, I wasn't popular at all. I was always teased about my clothes and hairstyles. I was always afraid to go to school because I knew the kids would tease me at breakfast, lunch and P.E. It was always, "I'm not your friend". if you are her friend. I never understood that because I was never a follower. I like everyone, but this one bully always wanted to run things, act like she was the ruler of everybody. I got tired of seeing her every day. I would tell myself one day I ain't gonna take no mess off nobody. I knew, I meant that in my heart, my mom eventually moved out of the projects because we couldn't even afford that.

At that time, my mom wasn't able to work for a long period of time or stay on the job for long because we didn't really have anyone to watch me and my sister without them mistreating us. I never understood why, but I knew when I got older, I was gonna work till I made it in life or until I couldn't work any more.

We ended up moving into this house across the highway from my grandfather, right behind my grandma's church. We lived there for a few months, which was the longest, hardest months of my life. My mom had three kids at the time. I was eight and my middle sister was three at the time. My baby sister was a few weeks old.

Things began to get harder. Seemed like we lived in a one room, functioning house because the other rooms were cold and not suitable for us to use. We had no running water, we only had a kerosene heater to keep us warm. We had a hot plate that had two eyes and one had a shortage in it. The little stretch we lived on only was two families. The neighbor had chickens everywhere in the front yard and in the back of his trailer. We would walk over there sometimes for my mom to use their phone.

When I tell you this couple was some type of characters, they were meant for each other. Well, let me tell you just a little bit about them. Well, the fella was my grandpa's friend and he would talk so much. You would get tired of listening to him. He looked like a real life caveman. I always wondered why he was bald and had so much hair on his chin. His beard would touch his chest. It seemed like it was always full of something. I used to wonder if he had lost any keys or anything. I was almost a hundred percent sure they would be in that beard. While the wife was my mom's friend.

So my mom thought she was probably four feet tall her whole life. She was short but spoke like a giant. She had a good heart but was still mean like a rattlesnake. She had a set of big eyes in her head. She was nice to my mom. A lot of times throughout our life and equally mean at the same time. We were used to everyone being that way toward us then. People would ride past us, see us walking and knew we didn't have a vehicle and would blow the horn and keep on going. I never understood why people treated us that way.

I remember on hot summer mornings, we would walk with empty milk jugs in our hands and my baby sister in the baby carrier. We would take turns carrying her as we walked to my grandfather's house. It was the longest walk ever to me and my little sister. Our shoes would flop off our feet. My mom's were old and torn as well. I could see the sun rays on the black paved road as we walked down the road. My mom would be crying and singing church songs to us and we would sing along with her. I would tell my mom, "One day, I'm gonna buy us a car and a house." She would laugh and say okay baby. My mom always made sure she instilled love in us even though we didn't have the material things. When we would make it to my granddad's house and fill up the water jugs we also would eat while we were there. My mom would find food for us only to find just enough to feed us with. My mom would look in the bucket my granddaddy used to give to the dogs the leftovers and eat out of that.

We would cry and my mom would pray. She would pray so hard she was a prayer warrior. We would sit a while before we went back home and normally wait for someone going back that way and catch them home.

My mom eventually joined a pentecostal church. That was in a nearby town. They would pick us up and bring us back home. My mom started to meet some nice people that would help us out sometimes. Things were starting to get a little better for us. It felt like years, although it was only a few months.

"My mom always made sure she instilled love in us even though we didn't have the material things...We would cry and my mom would pray."

-Sherida

2

The Fullness of Love

February 14th, 2022:

The day finally came and I drove an hour and thirty minutes to take my exam today. I walked in feeling like a winner, and sat down in the waiting area, happy as could be. It was Valentine's day. I had on my pink pumps, makeup flawless, my favorite blazer and pants suit. I mean like just dressed for success.

I went in without a doubt, said my prayer and kept on going. I was prepared in my mind. I was ready for the receptionist to tell me I passed. So I could cry tears of joy after sitting there and seeing how totally different the test was from anything I have ever studied. It began to make me sweat. I started to look around at everyone else in the room. I began to wonder if they were as nervous as me or if they were flowing through it with ease. I began to pray and ask God to help, help me through this and help me pass this exam and help me do it in his timing.

As it came to an end, I got up and walked out to the receptionist desk to turn in my pencil, my paperwork, and my scratch work. It was the longest few minutes of my life. Waiting on the test results to print out, only to find out that in that moment of truth, it wasn't my time to celebrate yet. The attendant looked at me as I skimmed over my results and said to me, "Did you do it? Did you pass?"

I grew emotional and tears welled up. And I tried to play hard and hold it in. Before I could get out the door good I cried. Tears were flowing so hard down my face. I felt that I had failed horribly.

♡ Rida

My mother and grandmother both attended church, but two totally different denominations. My grandmother belonged to a Baptist church, even though my mom was brought up in the same exact one. My grandmother belonged to my mom and was looking for her own place to belong. She felt her spirit and truth would come from a place where she knew she was comfortable with being herself.

My mom's church was the type of church where, when the holy ghost hit them, they release it and let go. They were seen running. Some members would even pass out and others put the sheets on them. I was always wondering why and what was going on, what was the reason for the sheets and them passing out? After a few minutes, they got up and went back to the normal church.

It was all different for me, but I enjoyed it. I ended up liking both churches. My grandmother was so sweet. She was different. She was mean too at times she was raised by my great aunt, her father's sister. Her mother was killed when she was a baby.

She was from sugar lock, Mississippi. My great-aunt raised my grandmother and my grandmother turned around and took care of my great-aunt. I never got to know the side of my grandmother's family. So it always left me in suspense. In my mind I would constantly ask questions like, *Who was I really? Who was I related to? How were they? What type of ways did they have? What did I get my ways from?* I had so many questions. Certain things would be going on with adults around me and I would notice it. I couldn't even ask them what was wrong. Everyone always said, "Stop asking so many questions." I tried not to ask so many questions as time went along.

After time passed, I was back at my dad's again. My dad wasn't the "church going" type of person. On Sundays at his house, you would wake up and it was just a normal day. Everyone was still doing what they were doing the day before and that's how I knew there was no church on Sundays there. It didn't even phase me to not have to get up early. That was a relief, even though I loved both of the churches I went to with my mom and grandma.

After some time went by my mom moved to a house in the same town as a church that she belonged to in a nearby town called Aliceville. She began to go to church often. We may have stayed in that house we first moved in no more than like six months. My mom moved a lot and we moved across town to some apartments in the same town. They were nice and the area was quiet. We were downstairs in the corner. No one could really see our apartment. I wasn't far from my school. All the kids at my new school, they were so cool. They were nice to me. I kind of knew some of the kids because my granddad's family was from a smaller area called SAPs. Most of the kids were my cousins. We would have so much fun at school, doing all types of stuff. The kids in that atmosphere showed me the new meaning of fun, like stuff I never even imagined doing. I didn't have to deal with bullying there at all.

I had one best friend. She didn't live far from me either. We would have so much fun together. She would stay at my house sometimes and we would hang out on the weekends. Sometimes on Saturday nights at my grandma's house, but my mom never let me stay the night at anyone's house. I knew the reason was because of the things that had happened to me in the past. In spite of that I could feel how things were different from me, I was starting to come along. I was starting to learn different things like how to act around certain people. But to be honest, I was already traumatized. Still sometimes stuck thinking about the things I had already been through in life.

Looking at those kids, saying, "I know they couldn't have been through half of the stuff I've been through yet." I was always watching everything around me at the same time my life was changing and I was so happy about that. Although I was still stuck in the past, replaying the things that shouldn't have happened to me and could have happened was on my mind. I was still that kid that had 1001 questions. I just knew I couldn't ask everyone questions like I used to.

I would have flashbacks of times when I did. My mom had this one good friend. He would pick us up sometimes and take us places. I can remember him being so angry when he would pick my mom up and he saw us coming, he would frown up to his mouth. He kinda looked like Jawanna mann. He would look at us with that lip turned up like we were contagious.

He was so hilarious to us. Me and my sister would laugh at him all the time. We knew he still loved us; he just wanted to be perfect to the T. And he didn't want you to mess up his belongings. He was so funny. Like funny, funny, everything had to be perfect to the if it was around him, his clothes, his car, his house, you name it, it was sharp. He would get mad as hell if my sister would wipe boogers on his seat. He kept wipes in the car and would pass 'em to the backseat while saying, "And keep them boogers off my seat." And if I asked him more than two or three questions, he would be hollering at my mama saying, "I'm tired of these kids!" My sister would kick the seat and laugh. He was angry because she was spoiled. She wanted to hang on to my mom's arm, and that aggravated him so much. But we had good memories of him because he made us laugh. Even though he was mean.

All those days of living in that little town showed us that even if we didn't have money, we still had love. Even when we still didn't have a car, we were still getting around, still learning new things, and still doing different things. And as you may have guessed, we weren't there for long. The time to move again came faster than I imagined.

My mom met someone and she was soon to be getting

married. We ended up getting a house. We had our own rooms and everything but her husband wasn't so nice to us. He was the type that wanted to control what we did and didn't eat. He was always gone so we were at peace while he was working. He had two jobs. So most of the time when he got off, he didn't want to be bothered with kids.

We lived right in his mom and dad's yard. Only thing that separated our house was a big tree. Just being honest. I never felt comfortable around any of those people. They were super weird. The kind you can't wrap your fingers or your mind around. He had a sister who was mentally challenged and she scared me at first, but after so long, I learned how to feel toward her. I was very compassionate toward her. She couldn't speak. So she couldn't express her feelings or emotions to those who knew what was going on with her or who had done anything to her. I would actually feel sorry for her. I began to learn more about myself and how I felt about other people. I started to feel others' pain. When I would be around someone and they were hurting, sad or angry I never understood why I would all of a sudden feel the emotions. That made life much harder for me because I didn't know how to control them. If you asked me, I could really tell how someone felt without them even telling me. I would watch certain movies and just cry.

About a year after the marriage began, my mom had taken all she could take from her husband. The last straw was him wanting to fight with my sister over some cereal that was ours in the first place. My mom knew that wasn't something she was willing to deal with. I never understood why an adult would even want to be that upset with the child about food.

After that day, moving forward, my mom gave us a long talk and it stuck with me. *"If someone doesn't like your mom, they don't like your kids and vice versa."* It was on my brain like a stain.

We ended up moving back to my mom's hometown in that same house by that saw mill. It was the one where you could smell and hear the machines all day long. We had an older car that time. It barely worked and certainly wasn't as nice as everyone else's car in town. I was super ashamed of our life and when mom drove me to school I would always ask her to drop me off behind the school. I was always scared or afraid that I would get teased by the other kids, and I ended up being right. I knew we didn't have the things like others but I was only ashamed because of the stares and bullying.

My mom stayed in this house with confidence that God was surely gonna make a way and we were gonna be alright. My uncles would visit us and check on us. We used to love to visit their house on the weekends. My uncles were so fun and cool to be around. I learned a lot from all of them, mostly everything I picked up and learned. I already knew I was gonna eventually master what I'd picked up.

My mom then started to let me visit my father again.

Things had changed a little, but he was still the same old mean person. The only difference was he remarried again and my mom hadn't met his wife yet. She was gonna be around me and my sister so it was important for them to meet. When Mom finally met her, she wasn't so nice. At first, my mom was mad at my dad for even bringing her to the house because of how ugly he talked to my mother over the phone. I didn't understand why my mom was so upset in the first place and why I seemed to have to be punished for it and couldn't go with my father. As a child I was clueless because I thought his abuse was normal. I cried so hard that day because she wouldn't let me leave with my dad. I honestly felt like it was my sister's fault but she was just a kid herself. She didn't understand. She never knew what was going on with them, and neither did I.

When my mom and dad went their separate ways and split up, my mom met my sister's father. Then my sister came along, my mom and dad were still married, just separated. So my little sister still was treated the same by my father as if she was his child. Even though he knew she had a different father as well. He never once treated her differently, but when he got married, things changed. He would pick both of us up and I could hear him and my stepmom arguing at times, she never really wanted my sister around if you asked me. I remember one night we were sitting in his car and he was gonna get ready to take us home. I could hear them fussing at each other. In my mind I knew it was because of my little sister. She wasn't comfortable with my dad continuing to keep both of us.

She came with children of her own so I'm sure she probably didn't want him to keep taking care of one extra that wasn't his. Even though it was never admitted, we knew it deep down inside. My mom stopped letting me go around again for a while. And I was so upset. Because kids never have any control over adults' actions.

My dad still loved my little sister and he remembers her birthday every year. He would call her his brown sugar baby and even my grandma on my dad's side loved her too. My aunts and uncles, nobody ever treated her any different still to this day. I was just happy that they never were mean to my sister. Literally she was like my first baby. When my mom had her and brought her home, I would get a chair and put it to the sink and try to help my mom clean her bottles and make her milk. It would be so soapy. But I loved my sister and my mom and wanted them to see me helping. I stayed close to my sister and when we were together, we would make up games and have fun by ourselves. Our mom always instilled love in us. Even when we didn't have money, she taught us to love each other. And for that reason, we always felt full and complete because we knew we had each other.

I smile at the memories of playing in the dirt. With my sticks, we would even try and copy our uncles except I was the leader. I would try and make fake cigarettes with dry leaves and grass then we would get in trouble. It was so funny to us. My mom would get on our behinds for that. Other times we would sit in the car and listen to the music on the radio. One day I told my little sister I would be back. I was going in the house and she stayed in the car. When I came back out she knocked the car out of park and into drive only to roll down the hill, through the fence, and into the cow pasture in our neighbor's yard. Oh my God. I was so scared. The car was rolling so fast with my sister inside and I was hollering for my mom. Mom came outside and my sister jumped out of the car right as it went straight through the fence. It was funny and scary at the same time, even the cows were hollering!

Those were the times when I was just living my life as a kid. Being myself and experiencing the fullness that pure love brings. In spite of our struggles and crazy circumstances at times, we had some good times together. We knew how to pray and we knew how to love.

" Our mom always instilled love in us. Even when we didn't have money, she taught us to love each other. And for that reason, we always felt full and complete because we knew we had each other."

-Sherida

3

The Loss of Innocence

February 14th, 2022:

I walked to the car on my way down the stairs of the building asking God, why? why? Why didn't I pass? As I drove down the road, I screamed at the top of my lungs, crying and hollering. You probably wouldn't have wanted to even be beside me in traffic. I cried so hard all the way down the road. It seemed like on this sunny day called love day on Valentine's it was pouring with rain. And my windshield wipers couldn't keep up with the rain. My life felt like it was just going to shatter. All to find out the person that I was supposed to be with was still entertaining somebody from their past. All of this in one day, I was saying, "Lord, I can't take any more." Nothing for a while. And I had to ask God to forgive me. And I didn't want to challenge God because things can always be worse than what they are. I cried so hard I could barely catch my breath. I began to ask God, "Why? again. Then I began to remember that anything worth having wouldn't be easy to obtain. If that day couldn't get any worse, I had to stop myself. Tell myself It's gonna be alright. It's already alright. I had all this come at me at one time. I pulled over and asked God, "What do I need to do? You show me, you tell me, I begin to tell him, I know it is in his timing and that I will have to work extra harder to make things better, to make things work. Everything else was going to have to work itself out."

As far as my loved one went I decided to fall back because what is meant to be will be in God timing not on rushed timing. As time went along I found myself juggling bills, having anxiety, fear of how this and that was gonna get paid. I even rolled over into the negative in my bank account. I didn't want to show the kids any red flags that I was stressed out about how the bills were going to be paid. I also didn't want to upset my publishers with my problems. I really didn't want to tell her I wasn't meeting my deadlines because I was stressed about my finances. I was getting behind on a masterpiece. I knew I needed to get this done, because this is my story. This is something that will help millions of people. People I haven't even met. people that I don't even know. I'm someone helping to change their life.

♡ Rida

As time went along, my mom started to attend another church. It wasn't far from where we live and our landlord was the deacon there. My mom knew him and his wife, so they invited us to their church home.. After the car went through the cow pasture it really put us down and didn't work anymore. So we started walking everywhere we went again. We used to walk around the corner to this older lady's house who was more like my mom's motivator or second mom who had a huge pecan tree. She was always stacking them up for us to take home with us. While we sat on her front stoop she would be giving my mom encouraging words and praying with her. My mom would cry to her and the woman would give her all kinds of advice. She became my mom's go-to person. It was always front stoop conversations. We would be out there for hours, sometimes until my little sister would be itching, crying and ready to go. We walked up and down that road visiting everyone she considered a friend or people she could trust. Most days we would sit on the porch and listen to the radio until someone came through that my mom knew.

After a while mom's landlord began to come around our house a lot. He was supposedly there to be fixing things but nothing ever got fixed. Like the back porch and the roof for instance, he was just hanging around to be nosy. (If you asked me). The old house we lived in had a large block cement porch. My mom would sit there and listen to the radio with us many of our days.

Our landlord was very creepy. He had a deep voice, like Barry White. He would scare you when he spoke and he was always trying to be nice by offering us candy. My sister never wanted to take anything from him. I would always take the candy. He then started offering my mom to take us to the stores and help with certain things like that. That's when I lost my innocence.

He began to take us to the store every other day. He started off telling me to stay in the truck and let my little sister go get what she wanted first. I would tell him that she couldn't go by herself because she was too young. He would say, "She'll be okay." One day things turned when he asked me if I knew who God was and I told him, "Yes."

Then he told me that it's important to keep secrets or God will take me to Hell. I know my face must have looked lost because he wasted no time explaining what and where Hell was. When he finished, I knew I didn't want to go there. I guess after that talk he felt secure to do whatever. I was gripped with fear of going to the wrong place and he used that as a way to remind me of how important it was to keep what he was about to do to me a secret.

After our talk he rubbed his big rusty, ashy, cracky, hands on my inner thighs and then said, "You go ahead and get what you want out of the store."

I was so confused about the conversation we had, and I

knew I didn't have any secrets. I didn't know what he was talking about, but he did. From that day forward, it was me in the devil's world, trying not to go to Hell. He waited a few weeks before he decided to put his hands on me again.

I remember when we went to that same store with my mom and pulled into that same parking spot in another old crappy car she was using that belonged to my grandpa. My heart was racing as I had a flashback and remembered what he said to me. My mom went into the store and me and my sister sat in the car. She cried to get out of the car and she couldn't that particular day. She threw a metal file and cracked the windshield.. They were trying to find the owners and my mom said she was in the store telling the cashier, "I'm glad my kids wouldn't do that." Only to come out and find out that it was my sister. She got the whooping outta this world.

Eventually, I asked my mom if we could continue to go to my grandma's church instead of the landlord's. Almost without hesitation she said we were gonna be going to this church from now on. We began to go to church with him and his wife every Sunday and some Wednesdays. Of course he was the one bringing us home and taking us there again since the crappy old car was gone. I was always afraid to look at him in his face but he would be sitting to the right of the pulpit with the other deacons. It felt like he was always staring at me. I would look away when he would try and make eye contact with me in church. I began to think he was a devil in church. How could it be possible for you to be safe in a place where you are supposed to go see God and the devil is sitting center stage just waiting for you to get there?

It was like he was always on a mission toward me.

"Why me?" was all I used to think and ask God.

That day changed me, and it kept getting worse for six months. He began moving his hands from my inner thighs to making hickeys on my chest. I hated to see him coming. He was still pretending to fix our old house, and it never got fixed. It got to the point where I didn't even want my mom to bathe us. She used to bathe me and my sisters in the tub together. But I just wanted to bathe in the tub by myself because I didn't want her to see the things that were on me.

He would park his old rusty truck on the hill beside our house. There were a few bushes that separated the hill from our house. I could hear the truck pull up. I could look out the window and see him coming. I wanted to cry, but I held it in and it took everything in me not to alert my mother. He would tell me to tell my mom that he was taking us to the store and my little sister would cry not to go. And my mom would say, just bring her some back.

I wanted my mom to say not today for either one of us, but my mom never had a clue. We would get in the truck and he would go down the road and pull over on this road by an old head start school. Each time he asked me if I remembered what he talked to me about. I would be so scared and would tell him, yes, he then began to tell me if I told my mom he would put us out. I knew then that sacrifice was mine to make for our house. I knew then that I couldn't tell. He would then bother me until he made me bleed.

As time went along, I felt like dying because I remember hearing the preacher talking about it being bad for people to do those types of things, and not be married. Plus I was only a child. He was old enough to be my mom's grandfather. I started to become angry all the time. The love I once felt was slowly being replaced with pain and after a while I decided I would rather go with my father and get cursed at and get whoopings than to keep dealing with being fondled and raped by our landlord, our transportation, and the deacon in our church. He pretended to be a Christian, taking us to seek the Lord only to be the devil when we got there.

I then started going back to my father's for the weekend. The shit he was saying, and the whoopings I was getting began to make me numb compared to what I was going through at my mom's house. I could never tell my dad because I knew I would probably get my ass beat like it was my fault that it was even happening to me. I started to drink my dad's beer in the red and white can so I could feel how the grownups were feeling. Maybe I wouldn't think about what was gonna happen when I got back home. After a while I wanted to drink every weekend. My dad said it was gonna kill the worms anyway. He just didn't know it was removing other worms and pains in my body, mind, and heart.I already at an early age thought my worth was gone, that I was a garden tool they talked about in the movies. I felt worthless. How could this be? I was only a kid.

As the summer months rolled in I found out one of my heroes was coming home from the military. It was my uncle. I felt no one could scare him or harm him. I began to pray and ask God to forgive me the same way I used to hear my mom pray. I knew I was going to tell my uncle. I was outside playing and saw his white Jeep come around the corner. I knew it was him because it had an orange and green tag and said Florida. My uncle effortlessly jumped out of his jeep with his uniform on and I was so relieved to see him.

The old devil landlord had just climbed a ladder to get on the house as if he was gonna fix some that he never even knew how to begin. I looked up to him and looked at my uncle. The look on my landlord's face was, " YOU BETTER NOT SAY NOTHING!" and I ran and jumped into my uncle's arms. I let out all the tears from the last six months and cried so hard in his arms.

He put me in the air and looked at me and asked me what's wrong. "Re-Re, why are you crying?" I began to tell him hysterically. My uncle put me down and started walking over to the devil landlord who was coming off that ladder so fast to get in that truck. I never knew what he said to him or how it turned out.I knew he left there in a flash because he knew he was wrong. Him and his wife told my mom I was telling a lie.

My mom told her what happened and she swore up and down that her husband would never do such a thing. She said he wasn't that type of man. I remember her loudly proclaiming that he was a man of God and she should be ashamed of herself for accusing him especially after all they had done to try and help us out. It was said that she tried to make me out to be a liar. My mom never got the police involved and he never bothered me or my mom again.

I was so glad when we finally decided to quickly leave that house. I remember looking back at the house and seeing my innocence stolen and left on the side, in that same spot where that old rusty truck used to park every day. I cried as we drove away. Trauma had replaced the happy, loving and free little girl with one that drank beer and was angry.

" I remember looking back at the house and seeing my innocence stolen and left on the side, in that same spot where that old rusty truck used to park every day. I cried as we drove away. Trauma had replaced the happy, loving and free little girl "

-Sherida

4

The Side Effects of Pain

May 1st, 2022

I gotta get a handle on this. I gotta take care of my business. I gotta let this stress go. I know stress is a number one killer.

I gotta find peace. I gotta get back by the water. I gotta get back working out, and doing what makes me feel best. I got to humble myself and go to work at a nine to five. This is what I have to do. Eventually things are gonna change, but this is what I have to do right now. Things are beginning to take a toll on me with my oldest child. My son will be graduating high school soon and I've had such a tight leash on him because the last thing I want to do is to turn the kid away that I had at fifteen years old. I don't want the world to take over and damage him. Trouble is easy to find, but hard to get out of.

♡ Rida

As time went along, my mom had moved a few more times and we began to struggle more, but through it all we had love for each other. We finally caught a break in life. When my mom got a job, earning a decent wage at a mental health facility, we relocated to a larger town that was closer to my mother's job.

I began to meet older kids that were nothing like the ones I grew up around. I had limited social skills, so it was difficult for me to make new friends. I was in middle school when we moved to Tuscaloosa. At first, being a new student in school with more kids than ever before was difficult for me. Overall, the kids in Tuscaloosa were nothing like the kids in Pickens County. I had to leave behind my only friends that I knew for the majority of my life to adjust to a new environment.

The difference between the kids in my formal school and new school was the fact that no one wanted to fight me or pick on me just because I was new in the school. I met my new best friends at this school. They stuck by my side and showed me the ropes in and out of school. We began to hang out after school and walked the neighborhood and sat around and listened to music. I then began to push my sister off for my friends. I didn't want her to follow me anymore. I knew I was wrong, but I didn't want to lose my friends.

My sister would cry to go with me and I would beg my mom to make her stay. The look in my mom's eyes bothered me, but she knew I was growing up. I didn't understand that I was breaking the bond between me and my sister. I knew that was something I really didn't want to do but it was too late. I tried fixing it but it didn't work. I felt bad but I continued to hang out with my friends even more.

Eventually, I ran into this guy who I thought was the finest boy in school. I had a major crush on him. He was so tall, in my mind he was 6ft tall although he wasn't really that tall in my eyes, he was the biggest and best thing smoking.

We began to flirt and talk to each other. Other kids in the neighborhood would say things like, "We're gonna hook you up with him!" My step sister would tease me all the time when he came around because she knew I really liked him but I was really shy. He had me in my feelings so I thought I would go to bed at night listening to Faith Evans thinking about him.

We never talked at school at all. It was almost like we didn't know each other. I would be so happy to get out of school in the evening and see his mom's car pull in the neighborhood and drop him off. I would stand on my porch and stare him down. We were five houses down but my 20/20 vision always kicked in for him.

This one summer weekend I remember him coming over to his friend's house across the street from me. It made it much easier for me to see him. I took the cordless radio on the porch and I would pop in that CD and play that song so he could hear it. I could hear him and his friends laughing about it.

I could hear them saying, "Somebody in love!' In all honesty he made me feel unexplainable. Later that same day the sun began to go down and the boys came off the porch and started walking so I decided I wanted to get a hug and kiss for the first time. We hugged and kissed that night and it was everything I imagined it to be.

I soon learned something about myself after that kiss. I didn't want to move too fast because of the past trauma in my early life. I sometimes wondered if others could sense what I had been through. We decided we were a couple after that kiss. I knew he was my boyfriend and we didn't talk at school but I didn't want him talking to anyone else. I was very territorial of him, but one day I noticed a girl that I'd never seen before over to his friend's house. She was acting like she was mad that he was over on my side of the street talking to me. She began to scream and curse out loud toward me.

I was confused about what was going on. She actually wanted to have a physical altercation with me about him. She lived a couple blocks over and apparently he was both of our boyfriends. So we got into a screaming match. My mother came outside and she was shocked that I even opened my mouth. She made me come inside from the porch that day.

I sat in my room and thought about things that day for so long until I thought my head would pop. My step sister later came in and gave me the scoop on the girl. She was actually my friend's cousin who went to another school. No one told me she liked him too.I felt like I had been set up. From that day forward it was over with. I couldn't see him the same. He became my enemy.

The first time we ever talked at school we had a physical fight with each other. The fight was about something related to a mama joke, but I had that anger toward him for being a player. I fought him like I was a boy. That's how angry I was toward him. He pushed me to not take interest in boys that weren't mature. I didn't even want to be friends with the kids in the neighborhood after that.

My mom then got an apartment on the other side of town. We lived close to a service station and the only thing that separated the place from the store was a fence. I would walk to the store almost everyday to get the same thing all the time. Dill pickle chips and Sprite.

I met a handsome young man much older than me and he had a job. The fact that he had a job stood out to me and I felt he was much more mature than the guys I knew. He was a junior in high school when I was in the eighth grade going to the 9th grade fresh to highschool.

He was so sweet to me. He treated me like a princess. He never forced me to indulge in sex. He would visit me after his shift and watch TV or sit on the porch with me. He was very respectful toward me. A year later it was time for him to graduate.

He told me he had decided to join the military and I was distraught. I felt abandoned all over again because I was losing my best friend. We started talking on the phone while he was away. When it was daylight, where I was, it was night for him. It began to be difficult for us to talk as much as we were. The communication line was fading away. He then stopped calling all together.

I cried, but I knew it was just how it had to be.

Shortly after our communication ended, I got into basketball and that took my mind off of him and feeling abandoned. I started being a part of different activities at school. Time went by and I knew in my mind that he may have found someone his own age that he could be closer with. I eventually began to stop worrying about him. I had a basketball goal and I put it to use every chance I got. This was one of the only things that helped. Every day I was out there trying to see how good I was and work on my shooting skills. I was working so hard one day when this guy came outside to the basketball goal and said, "You can't hoop!"

Although I wasn't that good yet I challenged him like I was the best at it. He was older than me too and he told me he was eighteen and I said I was sixteen. Truth was we had both lied to each other about our age.

He began to hang out at a relative's house often. That was the only way we would see each other. He would act like he was so interested in basketball, and how he wanted to train me with my basketball skills. I began to tell him about how I missed my friend, who was my first boyfriend, who I truly loved.

I can't lie, I slowly began to be intrigued by him. The flirting increased and before I knew it, I was getting ready to make the biggest life changing decision of my life. The first time we ever had sex, I got pregnant. I never even had a clue what to do with a child.

I don't remember much from my pregnancy but I do remember the delivery. Looking back on the day before I had to be admitted in the hospital to give birth, I remember saying to myself, *"This is it. This is either going to strengthen me or weaken me."* I was a kid, with a kid. I had my bags packed for my baby to come home. I was more excited about the cute outfits I could dress him up in and wanted to dress him up instantly. I had already decided what I was gonna put on him in my mind. I had my bags packed with all of my belongings and everything from the list the doctor had given me. I sat on the side of the bed and felt a little bit of pain as if I needed to go to the bathroom. I sat still staring at my bags focusing on them, thinking about how from that point on in my life, everything was going to be with a plus one.

How I was going to be viewed by others carrying a car seat, pushing a stroller at my age. I was scared. I felt my nerves go down my throat and into my stomach. I laid down that night in my room and stared at the ceiling in the dark, telling myself to get some rest. I thought, *Now this is your last day of peace and quiet.* I tried so hard to sleep and couldn't. My water broke a little after midnight and my family made a mad dash to get me to the hospital. I remember being rolled down a hallway in the hospital and even after working there, I can't find that hallway again. I remember my uncle/ brother was on one side and my child's father was on the other. Everybody was running down the hall to get me in the back. I remember them picking me up and putting me on the bed I was gonna deliver on.

I was having labor pains that hurt so bad for hours. As I laid there having labor pains while nurses were coming out of nowhere, constantly asking me to do things. It was all so new to me because I never knew you had to do so much before giving birth. I think I was more afraid of the length of the needle on the epidural than I was to push. When the time finally came, everyone was standing around my bed, waiting for me to deliver him. It made me very uncomfortable for people to be looking down there at my privates. My mom looked out the window. She said her nerves couldn't take it. She was brave to even be in the room because I would've passed out if I was her.

My mind raced as I began to push. I was hurting, thinking, and screaming all at the same time. The thoughts came quickly just as strong as the labor pains. *OMG, what is he going to look like? Will he be breathing when he comes out? Are they gonna hit my baby on his behind? Why is he playing Peek a boo?…come out already.* He finally arrived after many hours of waiting and wondering when it would all be over. I fell in love in a way I'd never felt before. It was a love only a mother understands. He was mine. I looked at him and he looked at me and I felt like for once someone was proud of me, regardless of my mistakes and things I had been through. I was in love.

"I fell in love in a way I'd never felt before. It was a love only a mother understands. He was mine. I looked at him and he looked at me and I felt like for once someone was proud of me, regardless of my mistakes and things I had been through. I was in love."

-Sherida

5

New Life

May 10, 2022

I found myself being so hard on him that I felt like I was taking his manhood away from him. My overprotective parenting wasn't allowing him to make nor learn from experience mistakes. The first time he made a mistake, I was so hard on him. I had to remember, my mama never gave up on me when I had him. So, I cannot give up on him for making simple mistakes.

I took his car from him. He lost his job that he worked so hard to get. And I had to tell myself again, really, it can be so much worse. Everything's gonna work itself out. I sat down, I talked to him one on one without yelling and screaming and fussing like I normally would do. For a while that's the only way I knew how to parent, because that's what my parents always did to me. And the more I yelled at my child, the more and more I hurt him, the more and more I found myself being more angry with my parents.

What stopped me in my tracks was the realization that I don't wanna drive a wedge in between me and my son, the way my father did with me. I just want to keep my son from the wrong crowd. I know my son is destined for greatness and I want him to embrace it and not let anything or anyone stop him or get in the way of him. I just don't want to be the one to push him over the edge into this world that loves no one. I apologized to him and told him I just don't want him to go through the things that me and his father went through. I can't speak for his father's absence or against him. My son sees the truth. I can only speak for my presence and not place blame nor create excuses, but to be a better parent to him for myself.

Things have gotten better, it feels like I am in a new life because I have changed the way I parent and live.

♡Rida

My son's father promised me that he would be better than his father was to him. I looked forward to that promise being a reality. I was still young and didn't even know how to be submissive in a relationship or even motherly at times. Women from his past were popping up here and there to constantly remind him of who was there first. I was a teenager and they were much older than me but they reminded me of highschool girls always trying to pick a fight. They would say things while he was with me and I began to view him much differently because I never once saw him get them in line or tell them to respect him or me. I never felt like he stood up for anyone or anything like he should have.

He moved in with me at my mom's house once my baby came with the plan to be there for us. I would work and go to school, he would leave and tell me he was going to work. I hated to see his so-called friend that would come and pick him up for work. He was sneaky and wasn't much of a friend now that I think about it. He would take him to do his dirt and also find a way to come back and notify me of what was going on. That definitely wasn't a friend. I knew he wasn't up to any good and thought he was gonna get somewhere by telling me these things.Only to find out the so-called friend was a relative to women he would come back and tell me about. I went into a state of depression thinking, *What have I done with my life? My life is over and I'm just here with a baby soon to have no help.* I would always have thoughts about alternate scenarios in my mind. *What if this hadn't happened or what if that my first love and I would've continued to talk. If my mom hadn't moved and I hadn't got a child, If I stayed close to him, if we would've even talked.*

I eventually saw my first love again and the look on his face when he found out I had a baby was priceless. I knew then that he would definitely not look at me the same. I went on and eventually I removed the what if thoughts out of my head.

Again, for the second time I had to tell myself, stop going back into the past and look forward. I was a master at beating myself up with thoughts and overthinking about what if what happened in my life was a reason. I tried as hard as my teenage mind would allow but always felt that no one my age would ever take me seriously in life. After several attempts of trying to make things work with my child's father, the best thing I knew was to just let it be and be done with it. I couldn't fight with him, too. I didn't know much about relationships but I knew I could be alone and unhappy. I didn't need company for that. I held on as long as I could but too many things were taking place over and over again. And I knew they weren't right. It was definitely time for a change. Me and him both was broken and needed to heal.

Adjusting to my new life as a mom came with the loss of many relationships and experiences. People treated me differently. People didn't want their kids around me and thought their family and their children were better than me because I had a baby. Although I knew they were doing more than I was. I was the one that ended up with the baby. Everyone around me in school thought I just went to another school. I never told them anything different plus I was ashamed to. Only a small group of my friends knew the truth because I saw them at my church. I didn't wanna add on to all the judgment that was being passed even though I was always taught only God can judge me. It still bothered me. Because I'm only human.

I got my GED shortly after dropping outta school. I didn't have to drop out of school, but that was the only way for me to take care of my baby and work and get the things that my child needed. Once I got my scores, they told me I had scored higher than anyone ever on the GED exam and it was harder than the exit exam in high school.

I passed because I believed in myself and knew I could do it. I always knew I was smart and I had to pass it so I could do what was best for me and my child. One thing my parents did show me growing up was to keep going and that's what I did. I got my first job at a local Sonic and my first apartment at the age of seventeen. My mom did everything in her power to help make it happen for me. I was determined to show everyone I could be a responsible mom no matter how young I was. This was my life to build and I did it without a car or any father present for me or my child. My mother and grandmother got me through it. Real love and support isn't based on mistakes or wrongdoings, and until having my son I had no idea of the battles I would have to fight in my new life. It was me and my son against the world with my mom and grandmother keeping a close eye on us.

Time passed and I created a new normal for myself and my baby boy. Eventually, I ran into someone I knew from high school and I can't explain why I felt so shy when I saw him. I think he was as shy as I was when the conversation began. When I saw him back when we were in school, I wouldn't even look his way. I felt like he was one of the kids that always laughed at me because I was big and pregnant sitting in a little desk at school. I also thought he was mean too. I told him how I felt and he told me he never judged me. Something in me believed it and another part of me didn't. I began to see him on a regular basis and he treated me in a way I had never experienced with anyone. He never tried to have sexual intercourse with me. (no contact at all.) We talked on the phone day in and day out. He did things for me and my child, and without me even asking he was there for me in every way you can imagine. I told myself that one day I would be his wife.

I have to admit when you're not used to that kind of love, attention and affection it can scare you. It will have you thinking, *Is it even real? What is your true motive?* But I didn't want to push him away. I was good at doing that because of all the hurt I had encountered throughout my life. All I could think about was not being hurt. Even through all of my doubts and reservations he continued to show me day after day, week after week, month after month, year after year, even after moving on with his life that he was still there for me. He showed me that his intentions were pure and he wasn't going to hurt me. Even after getting involved with other people and different relationships not working out, he never gave up on me. I watched him grow and get everything in life that he said he was gonna get. He is and has always been and forever will be someone special in my life. He taught me the true meaning of unconditional love. He never judged me for any mistakes I made. I would hang out with the wrong crowd. He still never judged me. Although we were absent in each other's life for a while. That king was the beginning of me being informed of how royal I am.

I don't know when it happened but something within me changed as I grew from an inexperienced teenage mom to a young adult. I began to leave my child with my mother more and I eventually moved in with the wrong crowd I was hanging around. Of course that led to me hanging out more in the streets more than ever. It got to the point where I just wanted to fit in with those people. Even though I wasn't raised that way. I was living with the people I thought cared about me, but they never really did. They were much older than me and looking back on it, if I was them, I would've sent my young tail home. Instead they welcomed me into a world I wasn't prepared for and played games I had no clue existed.

Out of all of them it was always one that did tell me to go home. I always thought he was being mean to me but once I got out of that lifestyle, he explained to me why he did. Me and him went through so much in life together. We would sit on the porch and tell each other how we had to change. That's exactly what we both did. It didn't happen in our timing but in God's timing. Till this day he is family to me. Blood couldn't make us closer. He told me how I helped change his life and that spoke volume to me.

My mom and grandmother would have flipped out if they knew about the long nights and short days, always up drinking, partying, smoking, etc, you name it. I was putting my own life in danger. My mom gave me time to get all of it outta my system and to not come back till I was ready to be there permanently.

I woke up one day and I knew I didn't need to be there anymore. It was time for me to get myself together and go home and be a mother to my child. The day I showed up to the doorstep It was one of the best days ever. When I came back home, my son was three and I was there to stay. My son and I grew up together. I went through so many life changes, moments, events before I grasped the concept of being his mother. When I did, I worked hard to prove how much I love my child unconditionally.

When I reached the point of wanting to grow up and really take care of business, the same person from school was still there to hold my hand miles and miles away while pursuing his own dream. I started working steadily and I landed a job in the plant. In my town, making good money was a plant job without a degree. That was the beginning of another chain being wrapped up in my life. I did that kind of work for sixteen years before I decided that all of the depression, anger, bad attitude and aggression that was coming out of me was coming from being stuck in a place for eight to twelve hours a day for weeks, months and years in years was too much for me.

I decided it was time for me to move on with a different journey in my life and that is just what I did.

6

Trauma Bonds

May 11th, 2022

I started a new job at a popular phone company. Everybody comes to get phones. The interview went so good. The person who was doing the interview is my supervisor and sounded like the perfect boss during the meeting. The moment I stepped in the door I felt like it was a competition because I had prior experience in management. During the interview, I just gave her a little too much information that wasn't even needed. I talked about my book. I talked about my specific days I needed off because of me trying to fuel the book. I talked about my boutique and how I wanted to relaunch. For my boutique, I wanna cater to the working women, to the women in the corporate world, to the women at these jobs, to the women that wear that particular attire. I also mentioned how I want to pass my real estate exam.

It was at that moment that she showed me this was a competition but she tried to mask it by acting as if she wanted to help me with my future.

I don't wanna feel like I ever have to compete with somebody I'm not in the same arena with. After that interview and accepting the job I made up my mind that I wouldn't stay long. I've learned that in every job, it's gonna be some of the same type of people in higher positions who will find a way to see you as a threat. They are the people that motivate me and push me to get on top of my stuff. Most times they are so caught up looking at others that they don't even see how they motivate others to achieve their dreams without even knowing. I use it as fuel when I feel like they are looking and pointing out insignificant things. I tell myself you got this. You gotta pass that exam. You can't work on a nine to five forever. You cannot stay there. I never again want to chain myself to someone's job that doesn't help me achieve my dreams. I've been networking then working, and I know everything is gonna work out in God's time.

♡ Rida

Life took a turn for me in 2015 when I met a new man that changed my life in many ways. We worked together at the plant in my town. I remember one morning we were getting off after working a long, twelve hour shift. As I made my way across the parking lot I walked and talked with one of my associates from work. He caught my eye because he was running late coming in on the morning shift. I saw him speeding up across the parking lot. He had long dreads, and was totally not my type, but it was like the sun shined on him that day.

We ended up bumping into each other the very next day. And I said, "Hey, how are you doing? You look like someone I know." And I started laughing but he was really short with me in the conversation. He quickly replied while laughing and then kept going. He ended up being moved to my shift and I saw him again. This time I said again, "You look like this guy I know."

And he asked me, "Who?" I told him, and he couldn't stop laughing. He said, "How could you possibly think I looked like that guy?"

I shrugged and said, "Well you do you remind me of him." That right there was red flag number one for him. He should have ran because I should never have told him he looked like somebody that I dealt with from my past.

After that we talked and we worked together. We were working in the station where we do cardboard. I would joke with him and I'd be like, "You're gonna be my husband one day."

He would laugh because I was straightforward, and came on strong. I think it was a little too strong for a female to crack a joke like that. But I guess that's what he liked about me. He was already seeing someone and so was I, but we were both having problems in our relationship. We would talk about the things we were going through. We would encourage him and he encouraged me. But those relationships played out real fast for us. We didn't intentionally mess up what each of us had going on, the people we were dealing with messed it up for themselves.

We just trauma bonded over and over again over the hurt. We acted off hurt in a vulnerable state to the point where we started looking for each other all the time at work. We worked in a plant where you had certain areas and worked within a certain timeframe. Things operated in blocks like round one, round two, round three, station one station two, station three. We would always switch with other people so we could work together. And we always ended up doing the same job so we could talk.

When we started talking to each other outside of work, he didn't give me his number first. I gave him my number and told him he can call me sometimes. So one day I got a call from this unknown number that looked like a payphone. I answered it and was shocked that it was him on the other end. He told me that he and the young lady he was seeing broke up.

I guess they had a pattern of breaking up and getting back

together but this particular time he wanted it to be his last time. The woman was still holding on thinking they were going to get back together because he'd already asked her to marry him. He told me he was leaving and taking his things back to his mom's house. He was no longer going to be seeing her.

I listened and told him, and when he paused I said, "This is such a coincidence because the person I was seeing, I helped get him a job then he kind of turned into a different person on me. He got his first check and went with the person he was with before." As I spoke to him about it I was thinking that the coincidence was confirmation for me and him to pursue each other. (Clearly I totally misread that.)

We finished our conversation and I said, "I look forward to seeing you outside of work." Shortly after the phone conversation came my red flag. One day he just showed up at my house and I don't even live in town. You can't just pop by and say, "Oh, I just was in the area and wanted to stop by to say hi." I live deep in the country woods.

There's no way I was supposed to be found without GPS or me giving him directions there. But he showed up and I was shocked. In that moment of being vulnerable I took it as if he really liked me instead of saying, oh, you need to run. We ended up talking more and began bonding because we were hanging out so much.

My birthday came and we dressed alike in our white

button down shirt with blue jeans on. My cousin and her fiancé were doing a little cookout and we went over there to celebrate. We chilled for a while and then he left me at the party. I ended up staying the night there and slept on the couch. I was trying to figure out why he left and started asking where he was.

Someone answered and said, "He said he was going to be right back but he was still gone." I wondered if it was because of the other woman he was with before me. I don't remember how long I waited for him that day but eventually he did come back.

When he walked in I could see he'd been fighting. His arm was wrapped up and he was bleeding. Immediately I panicked and asked what happened. He casually said, "Oh, I got stabbed."

I shook my head and said, "Oh no, this is not gonna work. This is not how things are gonna go. I cannot do this with you. Won't work." I paused to gather myself and mask my disappointment and a question flew out of my mouth before I knew it. "Are you actually getting physical with women?"

He was like, "No, I don't do that. She just won't leave me alone. She kept calling me, calling me, blowing up my phone. She even went to his mom's house where he was."

That made me furious and I sarcastically said, "So that's why you left." I think my mind just blocked out the rest of that incident because I don't remember the ending. I wanted things to work so I just left it alone. Shortly after that he was ready for me to meet his mom. It was so urgent to him and it came out of nowhere to me. His mom wasn't ready to meet me because she wanted him to marry the person he'd broken up with, which was totally not my choice. But it was put on me as if it was. This was another red flag for me but I was just so happy to have him and life felt good most days. After meeting his mom things started to seem official and we took the next step.

We began to be intimate with each other. I began to tell my cousin I wanted to take it a little slow and I didn't want to get too attached. At one point I felt like I needed a little space. Let me take you back a little. I always had this nice little shape with a nice little waist and small hips. I had on my waist trainer almost all the time even to work. I was very fit and at that time I wore a size nine or ten. One day while at work I had on some activewear pants and they burst. I stayed on myself about my weight because I wanted to keep it tight.

When my pants busted I instantly started crying and ran to the bathroom, and my cousin came behind me asking,u "What's wrong?"

I said, "I'm busting out of my clothes. Some things are not right. You know, it got me stressed out. I don't know if I'm gaining weight or these pants have shrunk." I was a little hysterical at that point and overly emotional but had no clue why. My cousin stood there with me listening as I paced the floor and kept talking. "I just got these pants and this is my first time wearing them." I told my cousin that my period hadn't even come on yet but it was time for it.

And she was like, "Oh my God, you think you could be pregnant?"

I said, "No, because last time I had sex, we used protection and we only had sex once."

After I said that she sighed and responded with, "Okay, you should be good. I wouldn't worry about it if I was you."

I wiped my face and said okay, and then we went back to work. The very first time we were intimate with each other, I got pregnant with my youngest son. When I saw the positive test I was kind of hurt. I said, "Lord, I got to make the best out of this. Getting rid of my child wasn't going to be an option." We were trauma bonded through the time we spent talking about the pains of our last relationship and I thought it was a genuine accident. Not knowing that the guy I slept with had told my cousin's fiancé his plans before we officially started talking. He thought I was nice looking and always wanted to talk to me. I never knew that because he kept it a secret.

He also never told me that he told my cousin's fiancé that if he ever got the chance to be with me, he would get me pregnant. I felt like that was low and when I found out about it, I was bothered. I didn't like that he made plans about me without me being involved. I went on to tell him what was going on and he laughed and told me it was going to be alright if I was pregnant. And I was like, oh no, pump your breaks. No, sir. That was not going to be alright. I didn't want to be another baby mama. I didn't want to be going through stuff without the father around. And I didn't want to have a baby and I wasn't married. I didn't want to go through that again.

As I told him that, he said, "Oh, I understand."

Eventually we decided we were going to be together. I was pregnant and he was happy. We got together for all the wrong reasons. We both had been hurt by other people. We both were going through things at that moment and we felt like we needed each other.

As Christmas was approaching he asked me what I felt about us taking the next step and moving in together. I told him that in order for us to live together we had to be married. I felt like he was in agreement but really only considered marrying me because I said that, which wasn't a great enough reason to be married.

Days passed and we went over to his mom's to take her a Christmas gift. When we arrived she had the girl sitting there waiting. Out of the blue the girl asked me if I wanted the ring he gave her. And said he still calls her and this, that, and the third. I'm like, Ma'am no, I don't want anything he gave you. That was for you. Cause what's for me is for me. And I had to tell her I didn't break them apart. She just wanted to place the blame on me at that moment. All she could see was the fact that he left her to be with somebody else.

His mom was sitting there trying to play the middle. At that time I was telling myself, okay, now I'm not going to go forward with this. Now I have to let him go. I stayed to myself for a few days then we started back talking. I told the mom how I felt about that, that particular day and that it bothered me that she would even do that. Looking back I can honestly say I handled myself well.

Two days later, we got married at the courthouse. It just felt like another day. It didn't feel special at all. It wasn't the fairytale wedding I'd dreamed of. And that was another red flag for me because I felt it was just something we were doing because we had to do it. That was totally not good. At all. We left the courthouse that day but I didn't feel right about the choice we made but I tried to make the very best out of it.

This was my first time being a new wife and I wanted to do all the things I thought I was supposed to. Growing up, I saw the women in my grandmother's church with their husbands and how they cared for themselves and how things were. I always knew I wanted to be one, and I wanted to do things a certain type of way, but what you don't know when you are a kid is that there are things that go on in people's households that you're not aware of. And that's when things get real. We had a lot of good times. We had a lot of fun together and he treated my children like they were his own. He did his best. He knew how or what he had as a parent as well. Because he experienced some hardships in his own life and we trauma bonded over that as well, our parents and how they did things. He tried to do his best and focus on the areas he needed work on.

I spoke on it and I would ask him all the time if he ever saw something I needed to fix or improve to let me know. He was one of those people where he would stay quiet, keep things to himself and he would just shut off. But once he got mad, he got mad.

I remember the very first time he put his hands on me. That shouldn't be a time or moment that I remember. I hate remembering it. I went and got my hair done and I will never forget it. Auburn was playing their rivalry team. Football is big in this town. When it came down to Alabama and Auburn I think everybody and their mama would be sitting in front of the TV or at least at the game.

Somebody wrote to me around that time and told me happy belated birthday that was taking place in November. This following year, it made him so mad because the person who wrote it was a guy I used to work with from Facebook. He didn't do social media at the time and thought that was a hindrance. (I totally agree to an extent.) Some people don't handle social media well, some people shouldn't use it. It can be a hindrance and a block sometimes.

So this person meant no harm by posting, *Happy birthday*

big head, haven't saw you in a while. It was all innocent.

We both had been drinking, but him more than me. I was in the bathroom fixing my hair and left my phone up front. I was in the mirror playing with my new hairstyle and just looking at it. He came into the bathroom to ask me about it. That's when I learned that some things weren't meant to come out of my mouth to him even if they were innocent. He came into the bathroom fuming, and I had a feeling that something wasn't right. When he opened his mouth to speak there was no love or friendliness in his tone. "Why did this man text you on here?" I was blindsided because I hadn't even seen the message yet.

I did my best to casually and honestly respond, thinking nothing of it, "It's Facebook." I looked at the phone he held in his hands to get a better understanding of what he was seeing before responding, "You know Facebook, it notifies you and all your friends of a person's birthday. That's how it goes. It's just a comment." It wasn't a private message but he took it as if I was smart mouthing him and being sneaky.

In his mind his response was justified because of the things that had been done in his last relationship. He was standing at the bathroom door initially then things took a sudden turn after I responded. It went totally left and he busted into the bathroom and started snatching my hair down. I remember him putting his hands on me over and over and over again. After what felt like an eternity and a million hits he knocked me over into the tub. I'd already been running water while I was cleaning out the tub to take a bath. The water was running. He knocked me over into the tub and I couldn't see but he was steadily punching me as if I was a man. This was the first time I'd ever been treated that way but it wasn't my first time seeing it. I saw it over and over again with how my dad did my mom. I never once thought I would be a victim of that.

I cried and begged him to stop but he continued to do it. I finally got up and I told him I couldn't breathe. It seemed like the person I'd met and married had left the building. It was as if somebody else had shown up in his skin. He told me he didn't care if I was hurt or not. Through my tears I told him I couldn't breathe and I was going to call the police. He told me if I did, he was gonna get out and come back and do it again. I went to my room and got in my bed. My baby was there. He was an on arm baby and saw everything. He cried as I was begging his father to stop hitting me, but my husband jumped up in the bed and stomped me with his shoes on. His steel toe work boots. It bothered me so bad. I was afraid and I couldn't go to work.

I used my vacation days for two weeks to heal. My face was messed up. I had to lie to my family and tell them I fell. I had a glass table. I loved that table so much. I got rid of that table just to make sure the lie seemed like the truth. I needed it to stick because I didn't want nobody feeling some type of way about him because that was my husband. My grandma was smarter than that and she wasn't having it. She herself had been there before as well and she knew something wasn't right. It scared me even more because he also took his vacation days to be off with me and make sure I didn't notify any authority or police department about this situation. It was so scary to me that that happened. At that moment I checked out of the marriage. All it took was that one time, my heart and my trust for the person that was supposed to protect me and love me was gone. He took that from me that first year of our marriage out of the years that we were married.

I tried to check back in on several occasions but I couldn't because I always wondered when it was gonna be the next time. I felt so much anxiety, always wondering if somebody was gonna hit me up from the past on Facebook or say something to me that would set him off. Even with the fear, anxiety and mental check out, I hung in there. I asked God to give me the strength to hang in there and continue the marriage.

But I was married to somebody I lived in fear of. Every time we argued and he couldn't handle or didn't like it anymore it would trigger him to put his hands on me or through the wall or drink more. That was too much for me, but I was afraid and didn't know how to leave until the fear became too much.

I was trying to get my walk right with God but he wasn't caring about his walk with God. I still made sure I went to church and did the things I could. I remember it being Easter and we prayed together as a family. He'd been drinking that morning. So he wasn't really praying that day and to be quite honest, I don't think he was really interested in having anything to do with praying at all. I always knew he felt like I was trying to force church on him.

That wasn't something he wanted but I wasn't about to let it come in between me and my relationship with God. We held hands and prayed. I quietly asked God to let his will be done in my marriage, in my life and to forgive us of our sins and everything we had been doing that wasn't of him. The smallest arguments were frequently turning into something so big and I feared we'd reached a place that our relationship couldn't recover from.

One time, I remember him packing all his stuff to leave. He was taking TVs and everything and when he left. I was worried because I didn't know how I was gonna make it on my own. That was one of my biggest fears and one of the reasons why I always hung in there. I would worry about how I was gonna pay the bills by myself on top of finishing school.

He wanted me to stop going to school anyway because he was tired of paying the bills alone. We agreed to let me go to school to become a nurse and some days things went smoothly as if everything was fine, but it wasn't. I started to work more because I knew he was tired of taking care of business by himself. He was a great provider and also a great cook. He was always at home, but sometimes people find the time to do and be just who they wanna be. He did, and when he did so did I.

That day on Easter changed everything. I was done pretending and I guess he was, too. I was talking to him, asking him a question and noticed he wasn't listening. I saw him walking away and then he began to yell and scream at me before going into the closet that held his gun. He did all of this and in front of my kids in a way I'd never seen before.

My oldest son stepped to him and asked him not to talk to me like that. I knew then that there was no turning back.

Before this day, my daughter had been traumatized to the point she didn't even wanna speak to him again. It was time to go, I had a choice to make and it couldn't wait. I gathered my kids once he got his gun because he'd been drinking and I ran into the car because I wasn't sure what his plans were.

He came downstairs, yelling, "You really think you're worth me killing. You think you're worth me going to jail. You think I'd do something to hurt you?"

He was standing in front of the car with the kids, sitting in the car looking at him. That was the scariest moment of my life. Whether I was right or wrong, I'd been traumatized from the very first time he put his hands and feet on me. There was no turning back, he broke it before we got into our marriage good.

I forgave him, but I still was fearful. And I knew after that day right there that I had to leave. I'd already prayed to God to let his will be done and that was the confirmation I needed to leave. And I did just that.

I think we became better co-parents than anything. We'd both been through things in life and my trauma bonded us on a lot of things. I he was raised by his grandmother. I never met her but I think when he lost his grandmother, things got hard for him. He married me and things didn't work out for me and him. I learned a lot during our marriage, the biggest point of advice I can give is, don't ignore the data. It's best to get data while dating and to heal before becoming one with people. Domestic violence has been dominant in my family. My great-grandmother, unfortunately, didn't make it through to tell her story. My grandmother and my mother both had to go away to battered and abused shelters for women. I didn't want the same for my life when it came to my marriage and I started to experience physical and verbal abuse. I prayed hard to God for guidance and asked him for his will to be done in my marriage and grant me permission out of my marriage. I didn't want to be the fourth generation of women to drop everything and leave my children to take cover for safety. God granted me permission to exit my marriage. Whether it be one time, or 20 times abuse is still abuse. It humbled me in a lot of ways in my life. A lot of people didn't know because I wouldn't share it, but I knew what the women before me endured from past relationships from broken men that hurt themselves. So they lashed out on them. When you pray about things, be specific and ask God to bring you out. I'm not telling anyone to leave. I'm simply just stating my experience in my prayer. This was my prayer:

Heavenly father,

Bring me out in good health and strength without hurt, harm, nor danger. Without me losing my life or anyone I love or my children in the process. Without me losing my mind without me losing my relationship with you or without me losing self-esteem and without me losing character. remove the very thing inside of me that the devil has attached. Renew me and help me be a guide and help someone else to make it out without losing their life, their mind, their self esteem or relationship with you. Heavenly father let your will be done.

Amen.

The saying is true, hurt people, hurt people. And when that happens things can get real ugly. Take your time and don't move fast is what I learned in that marriage.

Through it all I learned a valuable lesson to get out before it's too late or fix it before it even starts.

"I didn't want to be the fourth generation of women to drop everything and leave my children to take cover for safety... When you pray about things, be specific ask God to bring you out."

-Sherida

7

A glimpse of Hope

May 15th, 2022

It's funny how things happen! While preparing to write in my journal, I ran into an error message on my computer. It was telling me to free up space. I looked at it as it popped up showing videos and pictures from 2019 to 2020. As I was deleting, I ran across a video from the 29th of August in 2020. My father, my two sons and I were sitting on the back of my father's truck in his yard. He had the red carpet rolled out for us that day. He had the grill smoking, the tables out, all the meat, utensils, paper, towels, and juice for the kids. He was working so hard to try and impress me that day. When we showed up, he said, "I didn't really think you was gonna come, but I'm glad you did." I felt that moment that made him feel really good.

After watching the video five more times, I noticed that my dad was trying to make up for lost time all in one day. He was talking to me so calmly and putting in time with my boys.

I know you can't really go back and undo things, nor can you make up for lost time but knowing that he tried made a huge difference. All children need their mother and father, but a girl definitely needs her father. I can honestly say, hurt people, hurt people. It took me time, years, blood, sweat, and tears to understand that and to even understand him. He did to me, what was done to him. People display the things that they see while growing up. That is why it's important to break chains in generational curses. After crying, sitting and thinking, I can honestly say my father displayed his love for me the best way he knew how. That's why I forgave him for any hurt and pain he caused me in my life. That's a part of not only having a renewed mind but a renewed way of thinking and a renewed heart.

Those chains can no longer live in our family name, not on my watch. Those pains helped me grow to get to where I am and become the woman and queen that I am today. And I thank him for that.

♡ Rida

Shortly after getting my divorce, friends I had that had stopped helping me, who'd stopped communicating with me, started to come back around. I had this fear of being alone and paying bills on my own. How I was going to make it?

The trusting God eventually kicked in. I made it! I didn't ask how or why, but I made it and I was thankful for that. I did what I didn't know I could do or not on my own and I did it strongly. I ended up staying in our home for a little while longer. I applied for a new place that hadn't opened yet. I'd been on the waiting list and calling as long as I was married but I couldn't get it. I called and checked on the application over and over and over again.

One day I got a call asking if I was still interested in the place. I prayed, I jumped and screamed and hollered and I said, Lord, yes, I am. Before the call I'd been telling the kids we would move by Christmas. They smiled. I would say "you're going to have a bigger place. You're going to have your own rooms again." And God surely blessed us. Just as I told him he would.

We got a new home. Things were looking up for us. Blessings were coming out of nowhere. It was a glimpse of hope. Everything was looking good for us and I even started to get myself in check. I was working on my business, pouring into it and trying to stay dedicated to it; But sales weren't where I wanted them to be. The thing that helped me the most was the reality that I was working on it and I was happier than I had ever been in a long time. I know the boutique thing was something I always liked to do because I love fashion. I love clothes. I really wanted my own hat line. That was the goal. I knew one day that I would. I just wanted to add clothes because I loved to dress. My God sisters and others were always saying things like, you should design clothes. You are always so cute. Every time we see you, you know how to dress.

I wanted to decorate the mobile homes too because I love furniture. That was just one of my hobbies, fashion for apparel and furniture. I tried to get involved with things I love to do, and it brought me peace and happiness. Clothes were selling but I knew I needed to cater to younger people instead of just one particular type of shape or type of person. I had to cater to all. Eventually I felt that I was gonna need to take a break from the boutique in order to fuel it properly.   I wanted it to work and I will never quit on it. But I knew I needed to take a break from it.

Even with the break from the business, I was at peace in my home. My children were happy. Their smiles were smiles that I hadn't ever seen before. My children are so happy to be in their own space in their own home. I didn't have to worry about any hauling, fussing, hooping, and hollering. Having their own room made them peaceful and quiet.

Everything was different. I could sleep in peace. I was so happy just to be able to sleep in my bed at night alone. I got to the point where I feel like I could move on and keep on trying to build my dreams.

I always wanted to be a nurse. I would like to take trips to the hospital, just to go to the nursery and see the new babies. I always wanted to go. Whenever we were by the hospital, I wanted to see the new babies. When it came down to my next move it was either being a nurse, or to sell real estate. My uncle dated a lady when I was growing up and she was always dressed so nice. In my eyes it was so professional and she looked like such a business lady. I always said I wanted to be just like her. She inspired me to be the person I was gonna be, a realtor or a nurse. Maybe even both.

Time passed and I didn't get a chance to continue nursing school (yet), but I started to work on the second. And that was my real estate exam and license. As a kid I knew I wanted to have the biggest house. I would pass by the houses as a kid and imagine that it was my house. Sometimes I would even say it outloud "I'm gonna get that house." When I first started studying for my real estate exam COVID came and put a damper on things. The Kids were at home and they had to go to school from home. That's when things started to change.

I had to be furloughed for my job, and I stayed home for a while with the kids. The time was well needed. I could see the good and knew without a doubt that at this particular time in my life, I needed to be home with my kids. I needed to be able to help them with their work. Once COVID calmed down I went back to work a second job and everything was fine. Everything was looking up again.

The real estate prep course was tough because I was trying to do online schooling and make it through that. And when I tell you, I was so excited about finishing it! I made an eighty on the exit exam. For me that was confirmation that I was on the right track. I looked around at my life overall and things were looking so good. The kids were doing well in school. I ended up getting my son a car and of course he was happy. He was able to drive and I didn't have to worry about picking him up or dropping him off. It felt like miracles and blessings were flowing in my life. When I was off work for a while God took care of us. He didn't miss a beat of taking care of my needs and the bills were paid on time every month. I didn't miss a single bill.

God made a way. God didn't leave me. God kept me. I knew God loved me. I know I'm special to him. And I knew I needed to get all the blocks outta my way for me to receive what he had for me. Ultimately, nobody can get in the way of what God has for you. You can block it and hinder it yourself. I didn't wanna be a self blocker! I finally found that God is the way to make things happen. He has good plans for us and even the hard times can help us grow.

What I have learned the most is to always keep working on myself. I do this by being better with myself and others, by being gentle with me and others, and by making sure I operate in love. I work hard to operate with a clear heart and forgive myself for things I have done to people, things I have done to myself and things I have been a part of. Most of all I try to remember that everybody has a past, nobody is better than nobody, to keep on doing my very, very best. One day it will all pay off.

I'm blessed AND hope filled!

" Ultimately, nobody can get in the way of what God has for you. You can block it and hinder it yourself.

I didn't wanna be a self blocker! "

-Sherida

8

Break the Chains

April 26, 2022

I decided it's time to start speaking to myself better. I did an affirmation activity during my coaching session today and it energized me so much! From now on I will speak about my goals as if they have already happened. Allow me to reintroduce myself to myself!

Hello my name is Sherida Robinson and I'm a realtor and a new wife. I'm the perfect mother for my kids. I'm patient with my children. I'm calm with them. I'm slow to anger and my reaching is better

I'm going forward and getting better with how I perceive and receive things. I notice and understand my strengths and boldly practice them with no fakeness in my heart or my actions.

I am humble, letting go of trauma. and most of all, I am emerging and breaking chains.

Hello to the new me!

♡ Rida

I'm stronger than I was before. I now see myself differently and set big goals for myself. Others would never set these goals for me. Maybe it's because of my past or their low expectations but this is a must for me. I make next level moves for myself and my family to break the generational chains. This walk is not for the weak and people will switch out on you. It never feels good to be surrounded and still feel alone. Everyone won't understand you or they may act as if you are wrong about your thoughts and vision for moving forward in life. I couldn't care any less about the things they think or say. I get up and give my all to everything I do daily and so should you. I do what I feel like I have to do even if I dislike it with a passion. I work with passion because I have to do it for my kids and to make a way for my dreams to even be born.

This is one of the biggest chains I have to break in my life. I go to work and exist, all while thinking about my goals and my dreams, why I'm here, and what I'm doing it for. I know a traditional job isn't for me. It isn't my end, it's just one of my stops along my way. Growth will show you the things you use to get angry or upset about, but just let it roll off your back like water, and be humble. When you humble yourself, it pushes you to go harder for what you really want in life.

My desire to break generational chains and create a better life for myself is definitely my biggest motivator to go in and get off work each day with a smile when I want to frown. I get up at three A.M most days. That's my peace, my solitude, and my time to clean, pray, write, and to tell my heavenly father, my best friend and my protector how I feel thankful for the small things, and for my blessings that I haven't even received yet. I was speaking with my mom one day on the phone and I didn't want it to sound like I was complaining, but I started venting to her. She let me talk for a while then stopped me and said "baby, stop asking God for material things and for money. Try thanking him every day for what he has already blessed you with inside of you. Everything you need is within you." Those words stuck with me and now I pray daily throughout the day and tell him, thank you. In this season of my life it's important to keep thanking God in advance and expressing the desires of my heart. It's so easy to forget that everything we need is inside of us but it really is!

Our lessons come from experience and in each situation there is a lesson, sometimes you just have to be quiet to hear it. Sometimes it helps to mentally slow down your pace of thinking. Of course that takes a lot, but peace is a must. I go and sit by the water after I do my workouts, I walk in the park. And then it's easier for me to sit down and put my thoughts on paper because I have a clear head of all the things that hinder your peace.

When I first went back to work after my boutique I felt like my peace was disrupted because I couldn't do the things that gave me peace. Eventually I found a way around it on my days off. I was gonna make sure I went to the park and came by the water or get up at 3:00 AM. If I can't make those days, I figure out a way to find my peace while everybody else in the house is asleep. In order to break chains I have to find me and to know me. I have to go deep down inside, and this requires peace.

I know most parents can probably relate to what I'm saying. After starting my current job I asked myself what made me take this job? And in reality, knowing that I have to put food on my kids' table and pay these bills, I answered myself with hope because I know that it's better than no source of income. I remind myself that where I am is not where I will always be because I know what I'm destined for. I know this is just a part of my process. I have faith and I'm leaping out on it.

We have to stop hoping and wishing and just do it no matter what. That's when the change comes, it comes at it's time. Which is not always *our* timing. I often think about what my mom said and realize that she was right. Everything we need is within us. Everything I need is within me. I have to believe and trust in myself. And that's what I've been on my journey of doing. I'm breaking this chain and this is my developing process. This requires me to be more gentle with myself first because I have to nurture myself to make sure I get the best harvest. It's like a plant. A plant needs water to grow, plants need fertilizer to grow. I may not be able to go back and undo some of the roots of my plant but I can start now to nurture it better.

I took the development phase seriously and even started researching the active ingredients in what I eat. I started drinking more water and using things that make me feel better. Every day I get up and feel like my oxygen is better. My kids say, "Mama, you're mopping the floor again today." I laugh and say yes. The energy is there. The love for myself is there. I can get up and look in the mirror and feel like I'm beautiful. I'm everything I said that I wasn't months and months ago.

As I said many, many times before, I look at a lot of things differently. I used to cry and ask my mother what I did wrong. Why don't I fit in with certain people? Why is it that certain people and higher positions have more than me and still will treat me differently or act as if I was doing something wrong to them? If they were in a position to help, they never offered me help. For instance, I started an online boutique. I reached out to everybody I knew in higher places. And nobody wanted to help me. You know, it hurt my feelings. I would sit around and cry knowing people were in a position to help me, but they would choose to help other people. And I used to be like, why, why, why? Why not? I no longer give them precious mental space. I realize that sometimes you're just not those particular people's assignments. Sometimes whatever is meant for you doesn't include them to help you get it. Now, I appreciate all the nos. That powerful word (no) hits differently because I know things won't take off when I want them to, but they will take off. When it does I will not feel any type of way about the people who did not help when they could. I looked up to them in the beginning and I'm still gonna continue to look up to them because they helped me get where I needed to be. Those people motivated me, even though they broke me down a little bit, they pumped me up even higher than I was before.

My mom planted the seed that grew from my questions when she said "they see something in you that you don't see in yourself. And that poses a threat to some people, maybe not all, but some, or just threatened by your potential." I couldn't understand that at the time, but the more and more I transformed my thoughts and my way of thinking. I see a different level of myself, a different level of my thinking. I have to look in the mirror and get real intentional with myself and allow myself to reintroduce myself.

This new mindset is the mindset for me. You just have to tap in and value yourself, learn your worth and add tax. I want my big potential to turn into power. This mindset helps me to be proactive and proficient. I wanna stay in the highest mental space while doing these things and helping somebody else. You never know who looks up to you for help or guidance without even asking you for it. So be that helping hand. Move on and operate with love. Forgive people for sleeping on you, but be clear. There is no deal and no reason to be like them. Choose yourself first and surround yourself around people that are genuinely happy for you, because those are the ones who are truly for you.

I have learned not to be afraid of my bigger goals and making sure I set them high as I can. The first step is to visualize them and then believe them. If you can do this, you're definitely on the right path. Having high expectations of yourself isn't a bad thing. People used to make me feel like, *oh my God, how are you gonna do that? Why do you wanna do that girl, please? That ain't gonna happen. Blah, blah, blah!* If you stay small minded, you will always be in a small place. Have high expectations of yourself. Be intentional with yourself.

On my days of doubt or fear I remember I'm breaking those chains. I'm not perfect at all and never want to come off as if I think I am. But as a parent, I stand tall to my kids, even to my oldest who is taller than me. I'm breaking this barrier I have over my oldest child. For so long I lived in fear that he would make his parents' mistakes and that fear should never be projected on him. But as a parent, that's a battle we fight because we want the best for our children. I am one that knows all about making mistakes. I made many, and I know my child has to make them to develop himself because he's not perfect either. I learned to just tell him and my other children about my mistakes. First I make sure I have learned from, then pray for them and let them know.

I don't expect them to be perfect, but my expectations for them to be great because they're destined for greatness. Just like the potential that other people that look down on me saw in my life. I also see that in my children's life and I don't want them to surround themselves around people that are afraid of their potential or afraid of what's inside of them. I have learned that when you surround yourself with those types of people, it makes them uncomfortable. You know, the ones uncomfortable because of who you are. When you know you're making people uncomfortable and you've never done anything to them, it can lead to always trying to get reassurance. Especially if you are not yet comfortable with what's within you. Always seeking reassurance happens when you find yourself constantly asking questions like: What's wrong? You okay, what's up? What's wrong with you? Those questions do no good to anyone and won't help you get to your purpose or passion. This is why knowing yourself and knowing why you are living is so important. Make sure you learn a lesson with everything you do, get up and go hustle hard and succeed.

Going from being a mother at fifteen, to having a senior graduating high school, is one of the biggest accomplishments of my life. I couldn't see this far down the road, but I got to the top of the hill and I must say…everything happens for a reason. I was pregnant with my son while sitting in those small desks in school. He finished high school strong just as I wrapped up writing this book. I was by his side his entire senior year, holding his hand motivating him to finish his semester strong so he could graduate. When things were hard for him and adversity came along, he still came through strong. The teachers and the principals told me in all their time of teaching and being a principal, they'd never seen a parent come to the school and do all the things I did. I share this moment because as long as we are living, we are going to experience adversity. It's how we receive and perceive things that's most important. That's what I wanted my child to know and see.

It ain't the end of the world, just because you go through some things and make some mistakes. I showed my son that I'm gonna be by his side, and I'm also going to teach him what's right. That's nonnegotiable. I may not like it. You may not like it and it may not feel good. But I tell all my kids that, and that's one part of loving my children, having patience for my children. But that patience had to start with me first and now I have found different ways to communicate with my kids so they can understand me. Each and every last one of them has different personalities and I have to approach them differently. But I'm thankful I have been through everything I've been through. So I'm able to help them. I couldn't understand it when things were happening to me growing up, but I know how to protect my children because of that.

You train a child the right way. They will surely fall back on the way they were raised. They will not depart from it. My children are my biggest priority so I teach them right from wrong.

I teach them about the highest, our God. I teach them about our creator. I also teach them that nothing is perfect in life, so they don't expect it. I work hard so they know and see how to work for what they want and need. In life, that's what we have to do. Nothing is given to us. When I'm upset I sometimes want to yell at my oldest son because he's learning, living, and making mistakes. My mother would remind me that she had to do these very things for me, the same way.

Every step of the way my mother allowed me to grow up no matter what I did, she never turned her back on me. Even when I was wrong. She has always been there and that's a love I'm learning to have for my children. The parenting manual is never the same. It's an individual handbook designed for each and everyone. The handbook for parenting is truly created with pure and genuine love. The issues we go through can trip us up sometimes as parents. Many parents don't like to admit it but we have to ask our children to forgive us and bear with us while we are learning while we make mistakes. We also have to be bold and brave about correcting them. They need to know that as a mom or dad you will get it right for their specific needs.

The process I had to go through in my life has been long. But one thing about it, those are the things that made me who I am today. There is nothing (and I mean, absolutely nothing) anyone can say to me or about me that can hurt me or tear me down anymore, because those are those bought lessons. I wasn't spoon fed. I wasn't giving anything. I have seen and experienced a lot of things, but my trials and tribulations don't define me. That's what made me the women I am today. I can only speak for me because I have a peace inside of me that feels good. Not just on the outside, but on the inside as well. My journey will help others and teach others to believe in themselves. As a mother, as a daughter, as an employer, as a sister, as a niece, granddaughter, friend, coworker, son, father, brother, uncle, grandson, grandfather, or father. I don't ever want anyone to look at my confidence, get it twisted or look at me as arrogant. I changed into a renewed me. When I look at somebody else, I look at them as I look at myself, because energy is everything. And if we truly operate off love that God wants us to, we'll look at each other as ourselves.

I learned that healing is necessary, and you have to be patient with people while they're in their healing phase. Love is patient, my mom showed me that. I learned patience through someone else loving me. That person showed me the meaning of true love when I didn't think that someone could ever love me again. It taught and it still is teaching me to be patient with people who crossed my path without passing judgment on others. I don't want to do what has been done to me by others. That's another chain I've accomplished to break.

There was a time in my life when I was taking on more than I should. My peace was nonexistent because I kept feeling like I was running out of time to get the things done that I really wanted to do in life. That is the biggest mistake I ever could have made because always being in a hurry to do anything makes you crash and burn. I'm not in a hurry anymore. I'm not doing things in people's time. I'm not trying to copy anything. I'm simply doing me. I'm simply doing Sherida Robinson nowadays. I don't look at how fast others are moving and getting things done. I just want to do it right and create habits that are good for me.

Relaunching my clothing brand, the correct way will be the next best thing. I learned to stop trying to fit in with business people in the business world and just bring my world to the business. Sometimes taking years versus months is the best thing ever, just like with this book. I would not have known the things I know now to write it until now. This is what it feels like to emerge.

As I continue to break chains I build confidence in myself and the things God has placed within me. I encourage you to get rid of any insecurity and build confidence in yourself. It is not going to be easy because nothing great is easy to obtain. If you want something easy, then you don't want anything great. Greatness takes time and on the journey you have to protect and push your peace so you can emerge stronger than ever.

I protect my peace at all times. I had to learn that it was vital for me to do so. I learned a different kind of love for myself while pushing my peace. It's a kind love that doesn't require validation. I had to set boundaries in my life where I felt was necessary. And so should you. I had to take breaks and during those breaks, push your peace. You will get put to the test with no rest. Create stability in your everyday life. Push your peace. Be gentle with yourself. Peace should be customized to your life. You can't buy this piece. You can't be taught this peace. I'm pushing peace and encourage you to push your peace at all costs. It may require some major change, but it's necessary to cut out things in people that's only meant to be seasonal. That's what I have learned on the path to emerging and I hope you are able to learn it too.

" Peace should be customized to your life. You can't buy this peace. You can't be taught this peace. I'm pushing peace and encourage you to push your peace at all costs."

-Sherida

Sherida Robinson

Sherida Robinson was born in Tuscaloosa, Alabama, and grew up in a small town called Carrollton, Alabama. She's a proud mother of three beautiful children, Christian, Kiersten, and Andrew. Sherida has accomplished many goals. She has completed real estate school, was recently casted for a film by a top director and published her first book. She maintains her title as the CEO, owner and operator of Prolific lush boutique, while coaching others around her while remaining humble. Sherida is focused on creating a legacy for her children and continuously improving herself at the same time. She encourages self-care while pushing peace, love and faith.